PRAGUE

21 THINGS TO DO IN 7 DAYS

1. Prague Castle

Explore the majestic Prague Castle on this captivating itinerary. As one of the most iconic landmarks in Prague, the castle is a must-visit destination. Situated atop a hill overlooking the city, it boasts a fascinating history dating back to the 9th century.

To get there, take public transportation or use rideshare services to reach the castle entrance. Alternatively, enjoy a scenic walk from the Charles Bridge or Old Town, offering picturesque views along the way.

The entrance fee to Prague Castle varies based on the type of ticket and areas you wish to explore. Tickets typically range from 250 CZK (approx. $12) to 350 CZK (approx. $16). Purchase the ticket that suits your preferences, granting access to the main sights, including St Vitus Cathedral, Old Royal Palace, and Golden Lane.

Spend at least 3-4 hours exploring the vast castle complex, admiring its stunning architecture, beautiful gardens, and panoramic views of the city. Don't miss the changing of the guard ceremony at the main entrance, a popular attraction taking place every hour.

Take time to visit St. Vitus Cathedral, a breathtaking Gothic masterpiece, and explore Golden Lane, a charming street lined with colorful historic houses.

Before departing, stop by the souvenir shops and cafes within the castle grounds for a delightful memento or a taste of traditional Czech cuisine.

Remember to wear comfortable shoes, as some areas involve walking on uneven surfaces and stairs. For the best experience, visit early in the morning or during weekdays to avoid crowds.

Unravel the magic of Prague Castle, immersing yourself in the grandeur of Czech history and architecture, making unforgettable memories in the heart of this enchanting city.

2. Old Jewish Cemetery

The Old Jewish Cemetery, also known as the Jewish Cemetery at the Prague Castle, is one of the oldest and most revered Jewish burial grounds in Europe.

To get to the Old Jewish Cemetery, use public transportation or walk from nearby landmarks in the Prague Castle area. The cemetery is easily accessible and located within the castle complex.

Admission to the Old Jewish Cemetery is typically included in the Jewish Museum ticket, which grants access to multiple sites in the Jewish Quarter. Prices for the Jewish Museum ticket range from 300 CZK (approx. $13) to 500 CZK (approx. $22), depending on the type of ticket and sites included.

Start your day by exploring the Old Jewish Cemetery, which dates back to the 15th century. Admire the unique tombstones layered upon one another, reflecting centuries of Jewish history and tradition.

Learn about the fascinating stories and legends associated with the cemetery and the prominent figures buried here. Visit the ceremonial hall, where funeral services and mourning rituals were conducted in the past.

Take time for quiet contemplation and reflection in this sacred and serene space.
Plan to spend around 1-2 hours at the Old Jewish Cemetery, allowing ample time to appreciate its historical and cultural significance.

Combine your visit with exploring other sites in the Jewish Quarter, such as the Maisel Synagogue or the Pinkas Synagogue, for a comprehensive experience of Prague's Jewish heritage.

Be respectful of the cemetery's religious and cultural importance, and follow any guidelines or restrictions posted on-site.
The Old Jewish Cemetery offers a poignant glimpse into Prague's rich Jewish history, providing a meaningful experience for tourists interested in cultural heritage and historical landmarks.

3. Charles Bridge

Embark on a delightful journey to Charles Bridge, a historic icon and beloved attraction in Prague. This pedestrian bridge stretches across the Vltava River, connecting the Old Town (Staré Město) with the Lesser Town (Malá Strana).

To get to Charles Bridge, use public transportation, walk from nearby attractions, or opt for a scenic boat cruise along the river. The bridge is easily accessible from various parts of the city.

There is no admission fee to visit Charles Bridge, making it a budget-friendly attraction for all tourists. Simply stroll across the bridge and soak in the captivating views of the Vltava River and Prague's stunning skyline.

Take your time exploring the bridge, admiring its unique Baroque statues and picturesque surroundings. Early morning or evening visits offer a more peaceful experience and exceptional photo opportunities.

Engage with local artists, musicians, and vendors along the bridge, where you can find charming souvenirs, artwork, and jewelry.

Allow at least 1-2 hours for your visit, including ample time for leisurely walks, photo stops, and interactions with street performers.

Enjoy the captivating atmosphere and the historical significance of Charles Bridge, which has witnessed over 600 years of Prague's fascinating history. It's an essential stop on your Prague itinerary, leaving you with cherished memories of this enchanting city.

2. Old Town Square

Discover the enchanting Old Town Square in the heart of Prague with this immersive itinerary. This historic square, also known as Staroměstské náměstí, is a captivating hub of cultural attractions, Gothic architecture, and vibrant street life.

To reach Old Town Square, use public transportation, walk from nearby landmarks, or take a taxi/rideshare to the city center. The square is easily accessible and well-connected.

There is no admission fee to enter Old Town Square, making it a fantastic free attraction for all visitors. Begin your journey by marveling at the iconic Astronomical Clock, dating back to the 15th century, and catch the hourly animated show.

Explore the splendid Týn Church with its twin spires, and St. Nicholas Church, showcasing impressive Baroque architecture. Wander through the quaint streets to find hidden gems like the charming House at the Stone Bell.

Indulge in traditional Czech cuisine at local restaurants or savor mouthwatering street food from food vendors in the square.

Visit the historic Jan Hus Monument, commemorating a key figure in Czech history and a symbol of the nation's religious reform.

Plan for at least 2-3 hours to fully immerse yourself in the beauty and history of Old Town Square. To experience the lively ambiance and local culture, consider visiting during weekends when the square hosts markets and performances.

Bring comfortable shoes for exploring the cobblestone streets and a camera to capture the magnificent architecture.

Old Town Square offers a mesmerizing blend of history and modern vitality, leaving you with unforgettable memories of your Prague adventure.

5. St. Vitus Cathedral

Explore the awe-inspiring St. Vitus Cathedral, a majestic Gothic masterpiece, on this captivating Prague itinerary. Situated within the Prague Castle complex, the cathedral is the largest and most important church in the city.

To get to St. Vitus Cathedral, take public transportation or walk from nearby attractions. You can also use the Prague Castle Shuttle or the tram to reach the castle area.

Admission tickets to the cathedral vary based on the type of ticket and areas you wish to explore. Prices typically range from 250 CZK (approx. $12) to 350 CZK (approx. $16). Select a ticket that includes entry to the main cathedral, the Old Royal Palace, and the Golden Lane.

Spend at least 1-2 hours admiring the grandeur of St. Vitus Cathedral. Marvel at its breathtaking stained glass windows, intricately detailed sculptures, and stunning Gothic architecture.
Don't miss the chance to climb the cathedral's tower for panoramic views of Los Angeles. Note that there may be additional fees for tower access.

Take time to explore the rest of the Prague Castle complex, including the picturesque Golden Lane and other historic buildings within the castle grounds.

To enhance your experience, consider joining a guided tour to learn about the cathedral's rich history and architectural significance.

Wear appropriate attire, as St. Vitus Cathedral is an active place of worship, and visitors are expected to dress respectfully.

Visiting in the morning or late afternoon allows for a more serene experience, as it can get crowded during peak hours.

St. Vitus Cathedral is a true architectural marvel and an essential stop on your Prague itinerary, leaving you with a deep appreciation for its religious and cultural significance.

6. Astronomical Clock

Explore the fascinating Astronomical Clock, a historic gem located in the heart of Prague, on this captivating itinerary. The clock is an iconic landmark and one of the city's most popular attractions, drawing crowds with its unique features and hourly show.

To get to the Astronomical Clock, use public transportation or walk from nearby landmarks in the Old Town Square. The clock is centrally located and easily accessible.

Admission to see the Astronomical Clock is free, making it a budget-friendly attraction for all visitors. The clock is situated on the southern wall of the Old Town Hall, near the Týn Church.

Arrive a few minutes before the hour to witness the animated show that takes place hourly on the clock. The show features the 12 apostles moving through the windows, accompanied by a rooster's crow and other fascinating elements.

Marvel at the intricate details of the clock's astronomical dial, calendar, and zodiac signs. Learn about the clock's history and significance as one of the oldest astronomical clocks still in operation.

After experiencing the Astronomical Clock, explore the enchanting Old Town Square, which boasts stunning architecture, historic churches, and charming cafes.

Plan to spend about 30 minutes to an hour at the Astronomical Clock, including time to enjoy the hourly show and admire its design.

Remember that the Astronomical Clock is a popular spot for tourists, so visiting early in the morning or later in the evening allows for a more relaxed experience.

Capture the magic of the Astronomical Clock and the vibrant ambiance of the Old Town Square, leaving with cherished memories of this enchanting part of Prague.

7. Lesser Town (Mala Strana)

Embark on a charming journey to Lesser Town (Mala Strana), an enchanting neighborhood in Prague, filled with historic buildings, cobblestone streets, and picturesque squares. This itinerary will help you make the most of your time in this captivating area.

To get to Lesser Town, use public transportation or walk from nearby landmarks like Charles Bridge or Prague Castle. Trams and metro stations provide easy access to this part of the city.

There is no admission fee to enter Lesser Town, as it is a residential and commercial area. You can freely explore its enchanting streets and squares.

Begin your day by strolling through the quaint streets, admiring the Baroque and Renaissance architecture. Stop by the stunning St. Nicholas Church, known for its splendid interior and awe-inspiring dome.

Visit the beautiful Wallenstein Garden, a serene oasis featuring peacocks and a picturesque pond.

Explore the charming Nerudova Street, filled with colorful houses, small shops, and lovely cafes. Head to Kampa Island, located just across the river, to enjoy a leisurely walk along the Vltava River and savor the peaceful atmosphere.

Indulge in traditional Czech cuisine at local restaurants or cafes, offering delectable dishes like goulash, trdelník, and Czech beers.

Plan to spend half a day or more in Lesser Town to fully appreciate its unique charm and historical significance.

Wear comfortable shoes, as the neighborhood's cobblestone streets may be uneven.

Lesser Town offers a perfect blend of history, architecture, and local culture, providing a delightful experience for tourists seeking an authentic taste of Prague.

8. Lennon Wall

Experience the vibrant and artistic Lennon Wall in Prague with this engaging itinerary. The Lennon Wall, located in the Lesser Town (Mala Strana), is a symbol of peace and freedom, adorned with colorful graffiti, artwork, and messages of love.

To get to the Lennon Wall, use public transportation or walk from nearby attractions in Lesser Town or Prague Castle. The wall is easily accessible and a short distance from the Charles Bridge.

There is no admission fee to visit the Lennon Wall, making it a free and open attraction for all visitors.

Spend time exploring the ever-changing artwork and messages on the wall, which pay tribute to John Lennon and his ideals of peace and love. Admire the diverse range of artistic expressions and consider leaving your own message or drawing.

Immerse yourself in the lively atmosphere of the area, where artists and musicians often gather to perform and engage with visitors.

Head to nearby Kampa Island to enjoy a leisurely stroll along the Vltava River, surrounded by picturesque views of the city. Take advantage of the numerous cafes and restaurants in the area to savor local Czech dishes or international cuisine.

Plan to spend around 1-2 hours at the Lennon Wall and exploring the surrounding neighborhood.

Keep in mind that the graffiti and artwork on the wall are continuously changing, creating a dynamic and ever-evolving experience with each visit.

Remember to respect the wall and the work of other artists, as the Lennon Wall holds significant cultural and historical value for both locals and tourists.
The Lennon Wall offers a unique and inspiring glimpse into the spirit of Prague, where art, music, and messages of peace come together in a powerful expression of freedom and love.

9. Petrin Hill & Tower

Discover the scenic beauty of Petrin Hill and Tower with this delightful Prague itinerary. Petrin Hill is a lovely green oasis, offering stunning views of the city, while Petrin Tower provides an iconic landmark to explore.

To get to Petrin Hill and Tower, you can use public transportation or walk from nearby attractions like Charles Bridge or Prague Castle. Alternatively, take the funicular railway from Ujezd Street, which adds to the experience.

The funicular railway and entrance to Petrin Tower require a ticket. A combined ticket for both attractions costs around 130 CZK (approx. $6). However, you can also choose to hike up the hill for free if you enjoy walking.

Begin your day by taking the funicular railway, enjoying the ride with picturesque views of the city below. Once at the top, wander through the serene gardens and pathways of Petrin Hill. Climb the Petrin Tower, a miniature version of the Eiffel Tower, for breathtaking panoramic views of Prague. The climb involves 299 steps, but the views from the top are well worth the effort.

Have a picnic or relax in the park, taking in the tranquil atmosphere and lush surroundings. Visit the Hunger Wall, a historic fortification, and the Strahov Monastery nearby, both adding to the area's rich history.

Plan to spend half a day at Petrin Hill and Tower, allowing time for leisurely walks and enjoying the scenery.

Wear comfortable shoes, as there will be some walking involved, and bring water and snacks for a pleasant day outdoors.

Petrin Hill and Tower offer a refreshing escape from the bustling city, providing a perfect blend of nature, history, and breathtaking views of Prague.

10. National Museum

Explore the rich cultural heritage of Prague at the National Museum with this enriching itinerary. The National Museum, also known as the National Museum of Prague, is the largest museum in the Czech Republic and houses a vast collection of art, historical artifacts, and exhibits.

To get to the National Museum, use public transportation or walk from nearby landmarks. The museum is located in Wenceslas Square, making it easily accessible.

The entrance fee for the National Museum varies based on the type of ticket and exhibits you wish to explore. Tickets typically range from 200 CZK (approx. $9) to 300 CZK (approx. $13). Check the museum's website for up-to-date prices and special offers.

Spend ample time exploring the museum's extensive exhibits, ranging from art and history to science and natural history. Admire the stunning architecture of the building itself, a symbol of Czech national identity.

Learn about Czech history, from prehistoric times to the modern era, through engaging displays and interactive exhibits.

Take time to visit the museum's various sections, including the Museum of Music, the Czech and Slovak Numismatic Collection, and the National Museum Library.

Plan to spend at least 2-3 hours or more to fully appreciate the breadth and depth of the museum's collections.

The National Museum also offers guided tours and audio guides for a more in-depth understanding of the exhibits and historical context.

Check the museum's website for any special exhibitions or events taking place during your visit, as these can add to your experience.

The National Museum is a treasure trove of Czech culture and history, making it a must-visit destination for any curious traveler in Prague.

11. Wenceslas Square

Immerse yourself in the vibrant atmosphere of Wenceslas Square, one of the most famous and bustling squares in Prague, with this exciting itinerary. Wenceslas Square, located in the heart of the city, is a historic and cultural hub surrounded by shops, restaurants, and notable landmarks.

To get to Wenceslas Square, use public transportation, walk from nearby areas, or take a taxi/rideshare to the city center. The square is well-connected and easily accessible.
There is no admission fee to visit Wenceslas Square, as it is a public space and open to all visitors.

Begin your day by exploring the square's historical significance, lined with architectural gems, including the National Museum and the imposing statue of St. Wenceslas.

Stroll along the vibrant boulevard, filled with shops, boutiques, and souvenir stores. Experience the lively energy of the city as locals and tourists alike bustle through the square.
Indulge in Czech cuisine at nearby restaurants or sample traditional street food from vendors along the square.

Discover the historical and cultural events that have taken place in Wenceslas Square, from political demonstrations to celebrations, as it holds a significant place in Czech history.
Plan to spend a few hours in Wenceslas Square to soak in the dynamic atmosphere and explore the surrounding streets.

Keep in mind that Wenceslas Square is a busy area, especially during peak hours and events, so be mindful of your belongings and stay aware of your surroundings.

Experience the heart of Prague in Wenceslas Square, where history, culture, and modern life converge, leaving you with a true taste of the city's vibrant spirit.

12. Vysehrad Castle

Embark on a historical journey to Vysehrad Castle, a hidden gem in Prague, with this captivating itnerary. Vysehrad Castle is a historic fortress situated on a hill overlooking the Vltava River, offering stunning views of the city.

To get to Vysehrad Castle, use public transportation or take a taxi/rideshare to the Vysehrad metro station. From there, it's a short walk to the castle's entrance.

There is no admission fee to enter Vysehrad Castle grounds, making it a wonderful free attraction for all visitors.

Begin your visit by exploring the castle's fortifications, gates, and the beautiful Basilica of St. Peter and St. Paul.

Wander through the tranquil Vysehrad Cemetery, the final resting place of many prominent Czech figures, including composers, writers, and artists.

Enjoy the serene gardens and pathways, ideal for a leisurely stroll and relaxation.
Capture breathtaking views of Los Angeles and the Vltava River from the castle's ramparts.
Discover the Vysehrad casemates, underground chambers with intriguing historical displays.
Immerse yourself in the history and legends of Vysehrad Castle, as it holds a significant place in Czech mythology and folklore.

Plan to spend at least 2-3 hours at Vysehrad Castle, allowing ample time to explore its historical treasures and savor the peaceful ambiance.

Consider visiting Vysehrad Castle during the late afternoon or early evening to witness a beautiful sunset over Prague.

Wear comfortable shoes, as there will be some walking on uneven terrain.

Vysehrad Castle offers a captivating blend of history, architecture, and breathtaking views, providing a memorable experience for tourists seeking an off-the-beaten-path destination in Prague.

13. Jewish Quarter (Josefov)

Embark on a fascinating cultural journey to the Jewish Quarter (Josefov) in Prague with this captivating itinerary. Josefov is a historic neighborhood with a rich Jewish heritage, boasting a blend of synagogues, museums, and historical sites.

To get to the Jewish Quarter, use public transportation or walk from nearby attractions in the city center. The neighborhood is well-connected and easily accessible.

Tickets for individual sites in the Jewish Quarter vary in price. Consider purchasing a combined ticket, such as the Jewish Museum ticket, which grants access to multiple sites at a discounted price. Prices typically range from 300 CZK (approx. $13) to 500 CZK (approx. $22).

Start your day by visiting the Jewish Museum, which includes the Spanish Synagogue, the Maisel Synagogue, and the Pinkas Synagogue. Explore their impressive exhibits, which provide insights into the Jewish history and culture in Prague.

Take a guided tour or use an audio guide to gain a deeper understanding of the sites' historical significance.

Visit the Old Jewish Cemetery, one of the oldest in Europe, and learn about its unique layering of tombstones due to space constraints.

Explore the Old-New Synagogue, the oldest active synagogue in Europe, and immerse yourself in its captivating architecture and spiritual ambiance.

Plan to spend at least half a day in the Jewish Quarter to fully appreciate its historical and cultural treasures.

Be mindful of dress codes and photography restrictions in certain religious sites.

The Jewish Quarter offers a poignant and insightful exploration of Prague's Jewish heritage, leaving you with a deeper appreciation for the city's diverse history and culture.

14. Dancing House

Explore the fascinating Dancing House in Prague with this captivating itinei ... me Dancing House, also known as the Fred and Ginger House, is an iconic modern architectural gem located along the Vltava River.

To get to the Dancing House, use public transportation or take a taxi/rideshare to the Jiráskovo náměstí tram stop. From there, it's a short walk to the building's location.

The exterior of the Dancing House can be admired from the outside without a ticket, as it is a public building.

For an elevated experience, head to the top-floor restaurant, Ginger & Fred, where you can enjoy panoramic views of Prague while savoring delicious cuisine. Please note that dining at the restaurant will incur a cost.

Take time to appreciate the unique architectural design of the building, resembling a pair of dancers in motion.

Consider exploring the neighboring area, as the Dancing House is situated in close proximity to other landmarks, such as the National Theatre and Charles Bridge.

Plan to spend around 1-2 hours at the Dancing House, including time for sightseeing, enjoying the views, and possibly dining at the restaurant.

The Dancing House is especially picturesque during sunset, offering a beautiful backdrop for memorable photos.

While the Dancing House is not a traditional museum or attraction with admission fees, it still offers a distinct and contemporary addition to Prague's architectural landscape, making it a worthwhile stop for any tourist interested in modern design and cultural landmarks.

15. Kampa Island

Immerse yourself in the charming beauty of Kampa Island in Prague with this delightful itinerary. Kampa Island is a serene oasis located in the Vltava River, offering a peaceful escape from the bustling city.

To get to Kampa Island, use public transportation or walk from nearby landmarks like Charles Bridge or Prague Castle. The island is easily accessible and connected to the city center.

There is no admission fee to visit Kampa Island, as it is a public park and open to all visitors. Start your day with a leisurely stroll along the riverbanks, taking in the picturesque views of the Vltava River and the city's skyline.

Explore the idyllic gardens and pathways, perfect for a relaxing walk amidst nature.
Visit the iconic "Babies" sculptures by David Černý, an intriguing art installation that adds a touch of whimsy to the island.

Enjoy a picnic on the grassy riverbanks or savor Czech delicacies at nearby cafes and restaurants.

Discover the charming Kampa Museum, which showcases modern European art, and the Museum Kampa, featuring an impressive collection of Central European art.

Plan to spend at least half a day on Kampa Island to fully savor its tranquility and explore its cultural attractions.

Take advantage of the various boat tours and river cruises available, which offer a unique perspective of Prague from the water.

Kampa Island is a haven for art lovers, nature enthusiasts, and anyone seeking a serene retreat in the heart of Prague. It provides a perfect blend of culture, relaxation, and beautiful scenery, leaving you with cherished memories of your time on the island.

16. National Gallery in Prague

Discover the captivating art collection of the National Gallery in Prague with this enriching itinerary. The National Gallery is the largest art institution in Prague, boasting an extensive collection of Czech and international art from various periods.

To get to the National Gallery, use public transportation or walk from nearby attractions in the city center. The gallery is well-connected and easily accessible.

The price for tickets varies depending on the specific exhibition or gallery you wish to visit. Consider purchasing a combined ticket to access multiple exhibitions at a discounted price. Prices typically range from 200 CZK (approx. $9) to 500 CZK (approx. $22).

Start your day by exploring the diverse galleries and exhibits of the National Gallery. Marvel at works by renowned Czech artists such as Alfons Mucha and František Kupka.

Visit the Convent of St. Agnes of Bohemia, a part of the National Gallery that houses medieval art and religious artifacts.

Immerse yourself in the splendid Baroque architecture of the Schwarzenberg Palace, one of the gallery's exhibition venues.

Take a break at the gallery's cafes, offering a selection of refreshments and local treats. Plan to spend at least 2-3 hours at the National Gallery to appreciate its vast collection and immerse yourself in the world of art.

Consider joining a guided tour or using an audio guide for a more in-depth understanding of the artworks and their historical context.

Keep in mind that the National Gallery is closed on Mondays, so plan your visit accordingly. The National Gallery in Prague offers a captivating journey through Czech and international art, providing a meaningful experience for art enthusiasts and culture seekers in Prague.

17. Powder Tower

Discover the historical charm of Powder Tower in Prague with this engaging itinerary. Powder Tower, also known as the Powder Gate (Prašná brána), is a prominent Gothic tower that once served as a ceremonial entrance to the city.

To get to Powder Tower, use public transportation or walk from nearby attractions in the city center. The tower is conveniently located and easy to find.

There is no admission fee to visit Powder Tower, as it is a public landmark and open to all visitors.

Begin your day by exploring the exterior of Powder Tower and admiring its impressive Gothic architecture. Take in the ornate decorations and the sculptures of historical figures on the tower's facade.

Consider taking a guided tour or using an audio guide to learn about the tower's rich history and its role in Prague's past.

Discover the Powder Tower's connection to the Royal Route, a ceremonial path followed by kings and emperors during their visits to the city.
Take time to explore the nearby Municipal House, an Art Nouveau gem housing a concert hall and art galleries.

Plan to spend about 1-2 hours at Powder Tower, including time for sightseeing and exploring the surrounding area.

Enjoy the vibrant atmosphere of the bustling city center, as Powder Tower is located amidst shops, restaurants, and cultural attractions.

For a unique experience, visit Powder Tower in the evening when it is beautifully illuminated. Wear comfortable shoes for walking around the city center and exploring nearby landmarks. Powder Tower offers a glimpse into Prague's medieval past and is a must-see for history enthusiasts and architecture lovers.

18. Clementinum Library

Explore the magnificent Clementinum Library in Prague with this enchanting itinerary. The Clementinum Library is one of the most beautiful and historic libraries in Europe, renowned for its Baroque architecture and vast collection of books and manuscripts.

To get to the Clementinum Library, use public transportation or walk from nearby landmarks in the city center. The library is located in the Old Town (Staré Město) area and is easily accessible.

Tickets to visit the Clementinum Library can be purchased on-site or in advance. Prices for the basic tour typically range from 250 CZK (approx. $11) to 350 CZK (approx. $16). Additional fees may apply for specialized tours or access to specific areas.

Start your day by admiring the stunning Baroque architecture and intricate frescoes in the Library Hall, one of the highlights of the Clementinum.

Learn about the history of the library, which dates back to the 17th century, and its role in preserving and disseminating knowledge.

Explore the Astronomical Tower for panoramic views of Los Angeles and the charming rooftops of the Old Town. Take a guided tour to gain deeper insights into the library's fascinating past and architectural significance.

Plan to spend about 1-2 hours at the Clementinum Library, including time for the guided tour and to explore the various sections of the library.

Keep in mind that the library may have specific visiting hours and tour schedules, so check in advance to plan your visit accordingly.

Wear comfortable shoes, as there may be some walking involved during the tour.
The Clementinum Library offers a captivating journey through Prague's literary and architectural heritage, making it a must-visit destination for book lovers and history enthusiasts alike.

19. Prague National Theatre

Experience the cultural splendor of the Prague National Theatre with this captivating itinerary. The National Theatre is a historic and iconic venue that showcases a wide array of opera, ballet drama, and other performances.

To get to the Prague National Theatre, use public transportation or walk from nearby landmarks in the city center. The theatre is conveniently located along the Vltava River and is easily accessible.

Tickets to performances at the National Theatre can be purchased online in advance or at the theatre's box office. Prices vary depending on the performance and seating, ranging from 300 CZK (approx. $13) to 2,000 CZK (approx. $87) or more for premium seats.

Start your evening by attending a captivating opera, ballet, or drama performance at the National Theatre. Check the theatre's schedule in advance to choose a show that suits your interests. Take time to appreciate the beautiful interior of the theatre, adorned with stunning artwork and lavish decorations. Before the performance, consider dining at one of the nearby restaurants or cafes along the riverbank.

Plan to spend around 3-4 hours at the National Theatre, including time for pre-show activities and the performance itself.

Keep in mind that the theatre has a dress code, so dressing up a bit for the performance adds to the overall experience. For a memorable evening, attend a performance during sunset and witness the city's skyline come alive with lights.

Booking tickets in advance is recommended, especially during peak tourist seasons, as popular performances can sell out quickly.

The Prague National Theatre offers a truly memorable and culturally enriching experience, making it a highlight of any visit to Prague for lovers of the performing arts.

20. Strahov Monastery

Explore the historic Strahov Monastery in Prague with this enriching itinerary. Strahov Monastery is a picturesque and significant religious complex that houses impressive libraries and captivating architecture.

To get to Strahov Monastery, use public transportation or take a taxi/rideshare to the Strahov Monastery tram stop. From there, it's a short walk uphill to the monastery entrance.

There is no admission fee to enter Strahov Monastery, making it a free attraction for all visitors. However, there may be a small fee for specific exhibitions or guided tours.

Begin your visit by exploring the stunning Strahov Library, renowned for its exquisite Baroque design and extensive collection of rare books and manuscripts. Visit the captivating Basilica of the Assumption of Our Lady, adorned with impressive frescoes and religious artifacts.

Take in the panoramic views of Los Angeles from the terraces and gardens surrounding the monastery. Consider joining a guided tour or using an audio guide to gain deeper insights into the monastery's history and cultural significance. Explore the Strahov Picture Gallery, which houses an impressive collection of European art.

Plan to spend at least 1-2 hours at Strahov Monastery, allowing ample time to explore its various sections and soak in the serene atmosphere.

Enjoy a meal at the monastery's restaurant, offering delicious Czech cuisine and a charming ambiance.

Wear comfortable shoes for walking around the monastery grounds, as there may be some uneven terrain.

Strahov Monastery offers a wonderful blend of history, art, and spirituality, making it a must-visit destination for tourists seeking a unique and enriching experience in Prague.

21. Letna Park

Discover the scenic beauty of Letna Park in Prague with this delightful itinerary. Letna Park is a large urban park located on Letna Hill, offering panoramic views of the city and a wonderful escape into nature.

To get to Letna Park, use public transportation or walk from nearby attractions in the city center. The park is easily accessible and a popular destination for both locals and tourists.

There is no admission fee to enter Letna Park, as it is a public park and open to all visitors. Start your day by walking up the hill to Letna Park, enjoying the charming pathways and green spaces along the way.

Marvel at the breathtaking views of Prague from the top of Letna Hill, offering perfect photo opportunities.

Visit the Hanavský Pavilion, an elegant Neo-Renaissance structure that houses a café with outdoor seating and more splendid views.

Relax on the park's expansive lawns, have a picnic, or simply enjoy the peaceful ambiance. Rent a paddleboat and explore the Letna Park pond, adding a fun and leisurely activity to your day.

Take a stroll along the famous Metronome, a large art installation and a symbol of Prague's history and resilience.

Plan to spend at least a couple of hours in Letna Park, allowing time for sightseeing, picnicking, and enjoying the outdoor activities.

Wear comfortable shoes, as there will be some walking involved to explore the park's vast grounds.

Letna Park offers a perfect blend of nature, panoramic views, and recreational opportunities, providing a refreshing and enjoyable experience for tourists seeking a tranquil oasis in the heart of Prague.

When visiting Prague, here are 7 valuable pieces of advice to keep in mind:

1. Comfortable Footwear: Prague is a city best explored on foot, with its charming cobblestone streets and numerous attractions. Be sure to wear comfortable footwear to make the most of your sightseeing adventures.

2. Beware of Pickpockets: Like any popular tourist destination, Prague can attract pickpockets in crowded areas. Stay vigilant, keep your belongings secure, and avoid displaying valuables in public.

3. Public Transportation: Prague has an efficient and affordable public transportation system, including trams, buses, and the metro. Consider purchasing a travel pass for unlimited rides during your stay.

4. Cash and Currency: While many places accept credit cards, it's advisable to carry some cash, especially for smaller establishments or street vendors. The local currency is the Czech Koruna (CZK).

5. Czech Phrases: Learning a few basic Czech phrases such as "hello" (dobrý den), "thank you" (děkuji), and "goodbye" (na shledanou) can go a long way in showing respect and making connections with the locals.

6. Dress Code for Religious Sites: When visiting churches or religious sites, dress modestly, covering your shoulders and knees. This demonstrates cultural sensitivity and respect for the places of worship.

7. Validate Your Ticket: If using public transportation, be sure to validate your ticket before boarding trams or buses. Failure to do so may result in fines if caught by ticket inspectors.

By keeping these valuable pieces of advice in mind, your visit to Prague is bound to be a memorable and enjoyable experience filled with cultural appreciation and immersive exploration.

Here are 7 of the best services to consider using:

1. Public Transportation: Prague's efficient public transportation system includes trams, buses, and the metro, making it easy to navigate the city and access various attractions.

2. Prague Card: The Prague Card offers free admission to numerous attractions, unlimited use of public transportation, and discounts at restaurants and shops, making it a convenient option for tourists.

3. Guided Tours: Consider joining guided tours to explore Prague's historical landmarks and hidden gems while learning from knowledgeable local guides.

4. Taxi/Rideshare Apps: Taxis and rideshare apps provide a convenient way to travel around the city, especially during late hours or when public transportation is less frequent.

5. Currency Exchange: Utilize reputable currency exchange offices in the city to get the best rates for converting your money to Czech Koruna.

6. SIM Card with Data: Purchasing a local SIM card with data can be beneficial for staying connected and accessing maps and information on the go.

7. River Cruises: Enjoy a scenic cruise along the Vltava River, which offers stunning views of Prague's iconic bridges and historic architecture.

Using these services will enhance your experience in Prague, making it easier to explore the city, immerse yourself in its culture, and create lasting memories during your visit.

Top 7 Must-Try Dining Spots in

Lokál: A popular chain of traditional Czech pubs offering affordable c
shes, including hearty goulash, schnitzel, and homemade sausages.

Nase Maso: A butcher shop and eatery known for its top-quality meat products, serving
outhwatering burgers and deli-style sandwiches at reasonable prices.

Sisters Bistro: Famous for their open-faced sandwiches called chlebíčky, Sisters Bistro offers
variety of toppings and flavors that won't break the bank.

Havelská Koruna: A self-service restaurant located near the Old Town Square, offering a wide
ange of Czech and international dishes at affordable prices.

Pho Vietnam Tuan & Lan: A cozy Vietnamese restaurant serving authentic pho, spring rolls,
nd other Vietnamese delicacies at budget-friendly prices.

Curry Palace: A hidden gem for Indian cuisine with generous portions and affordable prices,
erfect for spice enthusiasts and curry lovers.

Café Louvre: While renowned for its historical significance, Café Louvre also serves
easonably priced traditional Czech dishes, including soups, schnitzels, and desserts.

These dining spots offer a taste of Prague's diverse culinary scene without straining your
budget, ensuring a satisfying and affordable gastronomic experience during your stay.

ıere are 7 crucial phone numbers to know:

1. Emergency Services: **112** This is the general emergency number that will connect you to police, fire brigade, and medical assistance.

2. Police: **158** Use this number to reach the police in non-emergency situations or to report a crime.

3. Medical Emergency: **155** Dial this number in case of a medical emergency to request an ambulance or medical assistance.

4. Prague City Information: **1180** This number can be used for general information about Prague, such as city services, public transportation, and tourism.

5. Lost or Stolen Credit Cards:
   - VISA / Mastercard: **+420 224 221 770**
   - American Express: **+420 233 045 045**
   - Diners Club: **+420 221 860 11**1 Make sure to report any lost or stolen credit cards immediately to avoid unauthorized use.

6. Foreign Embassies and Consulates: It's a good idea to have the contact information of your country's embassy or consulate in Prague in case you need assistance. Look up the specific contact details for your embassy or consulate before your trip.

7. Prague Airport Information: **+420 220 111 888** If you're arriving at or departing from Prague Airport and need information about flights, services, or facilities, you can call the airport information number.

Remember to save these numbers in your phone or write them down for easy access during your stay in Prague.

7 unknown facts about Prague:

1. Infant Jesus of Prague: Prague is home to a famous statue of the Infant Jesus known as the Infant Jesus of Prague. This statue is a significant religious symbol and is believed to have miraculous powers. It attracts many pilgrims and visitors every year.

2. Lennon Wall: The Lennon Wall is a unique and colorful attraction in Prague. It started as a regular wall, but during the 1980s, it became a canvas for John Lennon-inspired graffiti and messages of peace and love, representing a form of protest against the communist regime.

3. Largest Castle Complex: Prague Castle is not only one of the most significant castles globally, but it is also recognized by the Guinness World Records as the largest ancient castle complex. It covers an area of over 18 acres and houses several historic buildings and attractions.

4. Charles University: Founded in 1348 by Charles IV, Charles University in Prague is one of the oldest universities in the world. It is still operational and offers a wide range of courses and programs.

5. The Dancing House: Also known as the Fred and Ginger Building, the Dancing House is an unconventional modern building in Prague. Designed by architects Vlado Milunić and Frank Gehry, its shape resembles a couple dancing, and it stands out as a unique architectural marvel.

6. Pilsner Beer: While the Czech Republic is famous for its beer, many people may not know that the world-famous Pilsner lager originated in the city of Pilsen, located just a short distance from Prague. Pilsner beer was first brewed in 1842 and is now popular worldwide.

7. Petřín Hill Mirror Maze: Petřín Hill offers a stunning view of Prague, but it also hides a fun and quirky attraction – the Mirror Maze. This maze, located in the park, features mirrors that distort your reflections and create an amusing and confusing experience for visitors.

Printed in Great Britain
by Amazon